The Adventures of a Greenman Series:

Part 10

Raw Travel England

A True Story

By A. Greenman

Copyright©2012 A. Greenman
All rights reserved.
Published by Greenmans Books
in association with Lulu Press

ISBN: 978-1-4709-2104-0

This book is not based on a true story, it is a true story. Any resemblance to real people or events is probably intentional.

Cover Image by A. Greenman

The Adventures of a Greenman Series:

(in chronological order):

Part 1 Raw Beginning - *The First 30 Years of a Greenman*

Part 2 Raw Travel Brazil
Part 3 Raw Travel France
Part 4 Raw Travel Spain
Part 5 Raw Travel India
Part 6 Raw Travel New Zealand
Part 7 Raw Travel Wales
Part 8 Raw Travel Eastern Europe
 to 9
Part 10 Raw Travel England
Part 11 Raw Travel Crete
Part 12 Raw Travel Italy

Part 13 Raw Travel Europe (All European countries above)

Part 14 Raw Around the World Travel
   Parts 2 - 12 of the series.

Part 15 I Travel Light:
   The Man Who Walked Out of the World.
   (Epic formed of parts 1-12 and new material)

Other Titles by A. Greenman

The Practical Guide to Wwoofing:
World Wide Opportunities on Organic Farms

How to Take a Gap Life:
Sometimes a Gap Year is Just Not Enough!

A Greenmans Short Stories

The Wisdom of Travel
Words to Inspire

Introduction

Adam's parents had practically been modern day nomad's, moving wherever they found work, toilers of the soil and workers of the land. The young adventurer had known a dozen homes before he had become an adult. Taking up various occupations himself, before finally becoming a timber artist, constructing furniture and sculptures from reclaimed wood, in the old barn he worked from in the heart of the Sussex countryside, England. He had moderate success, his work appearing in art galleries, and selling. His face popping up on television and his pieces being commissioned by the rich and famous. However, something did not sit comfortably with Adam, he felt trapped in the rat race and was deeply restless in his somewhat questless state. Then inexplicably, in the year 2000, his work dried up. He had no money left and he had even borrowed to expand his business. What to do? This was the question, and a solution must be found soon. Adam remembered what a TV presenter had said about him when they reported his work:

"Alchemists have tried to turn base metals into gold for centuries. This man is a modern alchemist, whilst his raw materials are free, his work sells for small fortunes."
....but the question is, can he transform this situation? Can he reshape this dilemma?

The artist cannot settle, sleep does not come easily to

him, as he worries about his predicament. The year 2000 has come and by mid summer, Adam is at a complete loss as to what he can do. Yet strangely, one night, as he lies in bed in the small hours, he feels excited about the surprise card that life has played him. It has been a while since he had been commissioned to create anything, and a strange reality was upon him - he was free, in some ways, Adam had a blank canvass in life, in which to create on. Instead of battling with his sleep, he got out of bed in the middle of the night and sat, quietly, thinking. It was time, time to work things out. He was still, just breathing, waiting and emptying his mind...a few last thoughts came to him:

If I am completely calm, the answer will come, I know you life and I know you will help me. I am ready, I am here, I am waiting. Please guide me and show me the way.

It was a prayer, to whom, he did not know, but he believed that it would help and perhaps even be heard. Words came to him, ideas and he resonated with the potential that lie in them:

Alchemy. Chemistry's predecessor.
Elements interacting, transforming.
I can find a way through this, he thought.

He had always been enormously positive, but now he must call upon every ounce of the power in his mind. It was a serious situation, soon he would not have enough money for food or to pay for the rent on his workshop that had increased considerably, or for that matter, on the studio apartment that he now rented.

Adam sensed that he was on the edge of an enormous breakthrough, he did not know what form it would take, but he was certain that it would soon manifest.

This is not a problem, it is an opportunity. He told himself.

The question is, how would he react to it? More thoughts came to him:

Reactions to energy, that's all this is. Everything is energy, matter. Even my circumstances are charged with a hard factual reality. These facts too are energy. They have manifested in time due to the interactions of a complex scenario. It is life. It is my life. They are ingredients, that is all. If they are not giving the right result, then change them – use them. Step back from this, look at it.

At will, he removed himself entirely from the situation and a spark of inspiration shorted across the wonder of this moment. He felt expansive, everything was possible and he remembered other times in his life when he had felt this deeply intuitive perception, relaxed and thoroughly optimistic. So much so, that he even felt slightly 'out of this world'. Usually this level of inspiration led to the creation of a sculpture, but his pieces were not selling, there was little point in making more. He owed money now and had no work, this was a bad situation. He remembered a healer that he knew, who referred to his work as *Shamanic*.

"What is a Shaman?" Adam had asked him.

"It is someone who takes something that is bad and turns it into something that is good. We are not dissimilar in this respect Adam."

He remembered the ancient exercise which he often practiced, T'ai Chi, and how one could sometimes feel a tremendous energy during the gentle moving meditation. Adam saw energy as being malleable, pliable. Recently, he had been in a stage of stagnation. In Chinese philosophy, this was seen as a state of negative *Chi*. Expectation danced about the room he now sat in, his eyes still closed. A scene of planets came to him, playing before his eyes, small balls of mass. They reminded him of atoms, molecules, energy. He was curious to see where all of this was going, yet could not deny the feeling of hope which now dwelled within him, a hope that these ides would lead onto a solution to his deep rooted restlessness.

What if I could shift my situation, turn it around, move or remove the facts of my predicament, like balls of energy. Is it possible?

He was doing all of the right things, driven by a subconscious and primitive knowing. A certainty that he was here on earth for a reason and he would discover what that was and live it. It was 3am, Adam quietened his mind again, open to the realisations that would follow.

Payments, money, he thought. *What if I had no payments to make, no direct debits, no debt? Wouldn't that be good! How would I live, what would I do?*

They were good questions and begged serious answers. He would not let it go, Adam was driven and always had been. He recalled a phrase his maths teacher had once used:
"What if....?" It was designed to open the mind, provoke

one to think differently. The potency of the memory was enough to bring on another expansive thought:

What if I were to do something entirely different in my life? Adam dared to ask himself the question:

WHAT IS IT THAT YOU REALLY WANT IN YOUR LIFE?

And he knew it instantly, timing was everything and this was exactly the right time to ask the question...and know the answer.

Time. I want time. I do not have time because it always has me. What is the main thing that consumes your time? Work. To earn money. To pay for shelter, food and things that keep me healthy. Water to drink, to clean myself with, clothes to keep me warm. Fuel, to cook with, to warm my home and to run my van. Money to rent this studio apartment and for my workshop. What if somehow you could provide all of these things for yourself, cut out all of your bills and monthly outgoings? It would not be easy in England. Perhaps in a warmer climate it would be? I would like to find out, it may take time, but I would like to see if I could do it. A Gap Year would not be enough though. I would need to take many years, perhaps even a decade - a Gap Life!

Adam's realisation had been born. He knew it consciously now, he had always known it subconsciously, but now he had become fully aware of it. In time, he would see that this was a major part of his purpose on earth and the thought that there was indeed a reason for him living, other than to procreate, was a comforting one. What he could not consider for at least another decade, was that he was running away from life, there was nothing wrong with travelling and seeing 'the other mans world', the nomad would have a wonderful adventure, but the truth was simply not ready to reveal itself yet. The world was an easier place for Adam to live in when he removed the complicating factors that confused him, things which to most people were second nature.

Ever since he had been repeatedly beaten senseless by bullies as a child, he had often felt 'punch drunk'. A sense of disorientation had also increased when he fell off his bicycle and had a nasty accident, knocking himself unconscious. For example reading or writing, buying a pint of milk from a shop or asking what time a train left. It was extremely difficult for him to understand very simple information. He did not consider arriving in a foreign country and travelling by intuition alone to be an issue, for his sense of intuition was developing fast and would help guide him in foreign situations, in places that used different words. It would become a major factor in his life, language, when it was written in a tongue that he did not recognise, it would often cease to be a problem. As of catching buses, trains or buying food, there was much more leniency and patience shown toward foreigners, so Adam would mostly be treated with kid gloves. Beside, he was not even aware that he really had a problem yet, even subconsciously, it is a very hard thing for a grown adult to admit.

So the solution neared, to simplify life, reducing anxieties. To do this, he would need travel abroad. *Travel* that was the indirect answer to the question he had asked himself:

What do you really want in your life?
Time. Then what would you do with that time? Travel.
Yes, I have a vision to travel...see the world and live in the wild.

It was a curious solution, but one, although complicated at first, would finally yield results which Adam would never regret. However, there were obstacles to cross first, a lack of money, it was where he had started from, two hours ago, the problem had not gone away. No, but alongside it was now a dream, one that propped up his problem, in order for him to skirt round and examine it. The spark within was now a flame of a dream, one that he knew he could make into a reality. Adam could see it and so it became a vision, but how could he make it into a reality? Because he believed in it enough. Obstacles can stop you going forward, but you can also discover how to get over them.

Everything is energy, money is energy, he reminded himself.

What do I have that I can change into money?
Everything! He thought. *I can sell everything I own. My van, my tools, my possessions and even the goodwill of my workshop and the tonnes of driftwood* there. *I do not want things, I would like experiences! I can take the skills I have to create with me, for they lay in my heart, my soul and come out through my hands. I want to be free of these obligations I have, to raise so much money each week to live...it is too much. I will sell all that I own and make*

travel my home! I will even pay tax on the sale of all my business things, I can afford to with the losses I have incurred recently! There was no stopping him now.

Adam was not deluded, drugged or drunk, he was just determined. He would do it and do it quickly, there would not be a moment to change his mind. Hesitate and you give fear a chance to play its hand in the game of life and the vision of dreams, and he did not have room for that.

The potential nomad went to bed and when he awoke a few hours later, he felt utterly refreshed, free and inspired. The world seemed like a different place when he pulled back the curtains that morning...a world full of opportunities. What he lacked in academic achievement, he made up for with a creative resourcefulness, which would take him to places in life, both geographically and internally, beyond belief. Yet one day, he would believe it, as he will look back on the incredible journey which he would soon begin, a quest that would equate to as much acquisition of knowledge, as a Masters Degree may demand. His second step to freedom was in motion, as Adam's vision to travel the world as a journeyman, trading with his skills lit the coming weeks. The walker with joy moved at lightening speed to further fuel a catapulting start to his raw and hardcore adventures.

Within two months, he had sold everything he owned, except for a few small boxes of personal items. Adam had not yet decided where he would go, Australia, Africa or South America, it did not really matter, he was sure he could find his way practically anywhere. He was not only extremely resourceful, but also a practical optimist, who had achieved this goal to recreate yet another lifestyle by one thing alone, the right thought, followed by the right thought and so on.

The young traveller looked over the dates in his diary, to see how soon he could leave, and scribbled a note in the back:

Like attracts like. The most useful asset a person can have is the good thought. Have enough of them and you will be living a good life. It may take many lifetimes to build up enough credit in your karmic account, remove all traces of serious wrong doing, but when you do, the perpetual positive thoughts will accrue a staggering amount of interest.
Shopping list – BUY NEW JOURNAL.

Adam had invested wisely with his energy and intention in recent years and now his dividends would be paid. He had learnt that good things happen to good people, but so too do bad, or at least that is how they may first appear. It is just another type of circumstance, happening or energy. Energy that can be transformed into something good, the art is knowing how to do it. Adam did not really know, he just followed his feeling and somehow it seemed to be enough. This is what he would continue to do on his quest, his journey to return to nature and indeed a more natural rhythm in life. In time he would discover how to self sustainably provide for nearly all of his basic human needs. He had experienced an upbringing conducive to this way of life, his nomadic family had primed him well for the adventures that lay ahead and he had much to thank them for. Everything in his life had led to this point, it was a fact.

He was free to investigate all of the things he was interested in, all of the things he wanted to learn about and he would thoroughly apply himself in the pursuit.

When he walks into his local travel agents, Adam has still not decided where he will go. A colourful picture on the wall catches his eye, it is of a carnival in Brazil and the adventurer can imagine himself dancing there. Christmas approaches and flights may be scarce, but Adam leaves the travel agents with a six month return ticket to *Salvador*, Brazil. Anything could happen on his journey ahead and given the chance, it probably will. Adam opens his blank journal and begins to write.

To dream is to set the spirit free
When we dare to dream, against all of the odds
We give our soul a chance to dance
To dance through the ups and downs
For dreams can soon turn to nightmares
Yet we can look back later and see that we chose
Chose to take a chance and ask ourselves the question
What do you really want in your life?
Then we may just find the answer
It is then that sometimes a dream may become a reality.

Adam was a dreamer, however, he was also a dream realiser. He was beginning to unplug himself from the life he knew, prepare for an almighty leap off the grid and out of the system. Yet even dreams may be laced with nightmares when one looks deeply enough into the fabric of life. What he had not realised was that the further he went from all that was familiar to him, the further he would have to come back to that point. The path he had chosen would be an extraordinary journey and he must play out all of the scenarios that presented themselves, if he is to fulfil his destiny or utmost potential in life, but first, there were just a few more practical issues to attend to.

"I would like to cancel all of my direct debits please," Adam had particularly liked asking the bank clerk to do this. He was one step nearer to being off the grid and out of the rat race, he had nothing particularly against it, he just wanted to experience something else in life. Having sold his small driftwood business, the barn's contents and the goodwill of its rent, Adam handed in his notice on the flat he lived in. He paid off every penny he owed and bought his return flights and a back pack and would be leaving England with just £700 and no credit cards or overdraft facility. In fact, he would not even look at his bank account for six months.

Prologue

During that half a year, the wanderer stayed in a mountain community in Bahia and built a treehouse south of Porto Seguro, which he slept in for a while. After a short spell in England, he hitch hiked to France, got work as a carpenter, and with the money he saved, bought a bicycle. Cycling toward the south of France, Adam volunteered with the *W.W.O.O.F* movement (World Wide Opportunities/ Willing Workers on Organic Farms), staying in a yurt and learning how to make bread.

A summer in England saw a few more shekels added to his purse and the nomad set off for Spain. Over a period of nearly two years, he stayed in a ruin, taught T'ai Chi and made an enormous tree platform for a yoga teacher. The gold coins in his pocket rattled loudly this time, and Adam had a vision to spend the money on a fishing boat in India...and so he did, arriving in the mystical land with only a toothbrush and his passport. He bought a bicycle and begun cycling south. Successful in finding a boat, he set out to see, learning the ways of fisherman. All was well, until a tsunami came...but that tale we shall leave for another tale.

After Adam had recovered from his big wave experience, and earned a few more pounds for another journey, he set off for the wonderful land of New Zealand, searching for inspiration, hoping that the wild and raw nature he would meet would bring it to him...and indeed it did, detailed in his adventures in another part of this series. Having made a journey in such a vast expanse of pure countryside, Adam is drawn to be in similar places in the United Kingdom and settles in Wales for a time, warming by a log fire, building more wooden sculptures and roaming the valleys of the rugged land. All along, he is building up to one epic journey, to fulfil another dream. A wild and eccentric wish which is almost too good to be true...yet it is fact!

Adam wonders if he could renounce every single possession he owns, take his savings, which amount to less than one thousand pounds and without even a bag on his back or a set destination, head off on a spontaneous walkabout. Fuelled by a determination to fulfil his dreams, the wanderer does indeed set off and is gone for eight months, through Eastern Europe. Falling in love with a Hungarian girl, and having his heart wrenched from his being when they realised that they were not for each other.

When he does eventually return to England, in 2008, he begins writing about his journeys, on which he often volunteers with WWOOF. It is here that we pick up the story. Inspired by his land based adventures, the wanderer decides to begin writing about the many journeys he has had, before becoming a 'wwoofer' in his homeland. Volunteering with organic farms in England, he sets off around the country...this time he will be gone for eight months.

Raw Travel England

1

The call of the wild had been strong and Adam had followed his heart to test its way fully, wandering eastern Europe. Yet now, his desire to put down roots into the earth was a call which must be answered. It was easier for him to arrive in other countries with nothing, only trusting that life would show him the way, than it was for him to do the simple things in life, like buy food or turn on the tap for water. It sounded ridiculous, but all these things were just far too easy. Where had the challenge gone in life?

The free spirit had seen much of mystic matters and much more that he would never even write down in his travel notes. It mattered not now, for he sorely needed to move those gifts aside for a time and develop some of his other, more earthly interests. These things excited him and would soon become the backbone of his life. He had experienced raw simplicity in many places, but it was always masked with his excitement about unseen energy. It would soon be time for Adam to get down to business and move around a little closer to home. There was no doubt that the sound of modern man ran contrary to the peace of his soul, its noisy places vexing his quietness, but there were places, even in his homeland where much could be learnt about soil, trees, animals and other such natural existences.

No sooner was he back on the terra firma of England,

than he began planting fruit and vegetable seeds in trays. Taking his mind away from thoughts of his ex-girlfriend. She had taught him well, and the lessons had been tough, verbally thrashing him to the ground until his feet were certain to stay in one place long enough to become earthed again. Only, that place would not be Hungary, and the nomad would become 'grounded' without her company, shaking off the pain of lost love.

There is always enough going on in the world to help Adam forget about his own worries, life will bring distractions when we most need them. The next would come in the form of excitement, right on his doorstep. Just yards away from the flat where he stayed at a friend's house was the sea. It no longer rolled to the shore, as a ship had shed its load of timber some distance away. The lengths were strewn for miles along the coast, but at its thickest it lay six feet high and ten feet deep, floating at the place where waves would normally break. In just a few hours, nature had turned over a cargo ship and spread its goods all over the beaches of Sussex. When man has forgotten that the will of nature is supreme, it will shake him to the ground with a display of its power.

Adam stands looking at the great sight, the haunting tombs of timber, rising up in the sea, like one solid mass of corpses in the water. He draws a long slow breath, the cool salty spray clears his nose. The timber artist does not collect this squared material to use, it does not inspire him in this way, but many people do, against the will of the law. Instead, it soothes him as he gazes upon the teams of machines that fight to clear up the piles, forcing the beach to be closed to the wandering public for months.

When the sea is closed, one must take heed to the message given, so Adam does not try and travel away from the Land of Eng. He cannot really, inside he is broken, his recent months have jolted him severely.

Why do I do such things? He asks himself.
To travel with nothing, following only my intuition? Perhaps to feel alive? I wonder how near to home I can stay this time and for how long? Where is home for me? He wonders.

Like the spill of the timber cargo, sometimes damage happens. This is a time of damage. It is a lesson of the heart, his is splintered and is a sorry sight for a while. Wounded, with no hope, joy or peace. Adam carries on planting seeds in little pots, until he finds a garden where he can plant his tomatoes, pumpkins, lettuces, peppers and potatoes. The simplicity of the action holds him together, in one piece.

Now, he must find a place to settle, he is not in a state to go anywhere for quite some time. He is unsure of how to go about finding a home, as he cannot afford to rent his own place and he certainly would not consider receiving *Housing Benefit* now.

The wanderer returns to an old T'ai Chi group and luck plays its hand once again. A friend approaches him and says:

"I heard that you could do with a place to live Adam."

"Yes that's right, I could," he replies, a little surprised.

"Well I have a flat that you could stay in, it's not up to much and we will need to put in a kitchen, it doesn't really have much of one at the moment, but I am sure we could come to an amicable arrangement," he suggests.

"Oh that's wonderful, thank you. Where is it?" Adam asks.

"Do you know Garden Mansions, on Garden Terrace? It's along there, at the back of the building on the third floor, facing north."

"Yes I do know Garden Terrace, I used to live there with my girlfriend until 1999. Well I'll be! A full circle, nearly ten years later I've come back to where I left from!"

Naturally, Adam accepts the kind offer, lent heavily in his favour. The place had been left to his friend by some dear old friends of his who had passed away. It is absolutely choc-o-block with their belongings, but it is warm, dry and comfortable and just what Adam needs.

In time, Adam will go through the place and clear out all the old things that are not wanted and clean up the whole flat right through. Many other items he moves up into its loft and gives him self a little bit more room. The activity helps him focus on a life without travel, but he will still need to earn a few shekels to see him through this strange period, and takes the first job he can find. It is to be a porter at the local hospital, a huge place with many a distraction, and it is a good reason to get up every morning. The job cheers him up and as he does it, he writes, on any scrap of paper he can find. Every spare moment that he has would be spent jotting down a few more fragments of information, a memory or an image from his travels.

This won't do, he told himself.

One day I will have to write this lot up and then I will throw away all the scraps once the job is done.

There were memories coming up from all through his life, the many countries he had stayed in. The nomadic porter makes his way up to his birth place, the massive old farm where he was born. Somehow, he needs to make sense of his life, and this is a good place to begin.

What has happened? What has led me to this time in my life? And what led me to leave Wales with nothing and go through so many countries? Was it to meet my girlfriend, who would indirectly bring me back to earth with such a bang? I believe so.

He does not really understand everything, but he does not have to, he is here, in England, safe and well. All he really wants to do is write, there is so much to bring out, so much to record, understand and then move on from.

When he had earned enough money at the hospital and his temporary contract had come to an end, Adam did not try to renew it, he has other plans. It has been an incredible experience being there, particularly as his job involved throwing out rubbish. He saw how much was thrown away, equipment that had cost thousands and thousands of pounds just a handful of years before. Now, obsolete, deemed a security issue to sell on, as someone may sue the NHS for damages if they had a problem with it. Adam practically built his own clinic in the basement, with all the stuff that was thrown out daily.

Like a caged animal, he looks out of the high buildings that he works in, just dying to stretch his legs upon the rolling green hills that he can see. It looks very much like freedom to him and reminds Adam that he is as free as he allowed his mind to be. So just for fun, he tries out his favourite question:

What is it that you really want to do in your life?

It was not difficult to know.

I would just love to write up my memories of travel, notes and thoughts. What is stopping me doing this right now? Nothing, he thought.

The chances of him staying around for long were remote. Though right now, he could and he wrote until his heart was content and gradually it was becoming so. Then as he came toward the end of jotting down all he wished, for the time being, he guessed that life must have a new stage in store for him and indeed it did. The wanderer had thought much about the voluntary work he had participated in over the years and turned his attention to finding some in England...in between getting his lat few words out, for now.

Life is a cycle made up of change. The links of time are like that of a bicycle, sometimes they break, sometimes the chain falls off. Other times it will run dry and on odd occasions spoil our clothes. At the same time, it is a mechanism that works, if in tune, with all that is around it; the crank, the gears and the rider. The same for the human, he or she may also experience a bump in the ride, but if you fall off, you can get back on. It may take a day, a week or years. Like the bicycle, the human may find balance again and continue toward his or her destination, of course, it is an endless road, its destination being the cycle of life.

Once again, the man of the land volunteered with the *Wwoof* movement, first of all, on farms nearby and then on some of the many others around the country. It was September, a wonderful time to work in the English countryside. There were hundreds of opportunities on organic farms around England and Adam began to plot a course for the coming months. He had left the seafront flat for now, and was on the road again, and the idea of not knowing how long he would be gone or what may happen thrilled him. He had done much 'wwoofing' over the years and it always made him feel at peace. Through his work he began to heal the imbalance that he still felt from time to time, from his relatively recent loss of love. As he sowed seeds into the land, he also sewed back together the pieces of his broken heart. For when he loved, he really loved and when he lost, he lost. It would not always be so, but the wanderer was still finding his way.

He did not need to go far in order to reach his first destination, for it was in his home county of Sussex. The wwoofer began by helping to restore an old gypsy wagon, removing some of the rotten one hundred and fifty year old timbers. At other times he dug trenches for the electric cables that would light this old travellers dwelling. He was helped by another wwoofer from Germany, and Adam found that his trench digging was very precise and time consuming, he could not stand to get any soil on his clothes and was always immaculate at the end of a days work...until Adam smeared mud on him.

The simplicity of the work was almost sacred to the wanderer, as he volunteered on farms, in exchange for his bed, board and infinite possibilities to learn about the land. On others, he would learn more about animals, livestock and the food that is grown to meet our basic human needs. Such delight is known to few men in the grand scheme of things, in the fast and frantic world that we live in, one that Adam found it hard to be in. Yet in time, his work on the land would also bring him back down to earth.

Ever since Adam had been beaten senseless as a child, bullied and knocked unconscious, he often felt punch trunk. He still had difficulty processing information, so when his wwoof host began giving him the jobs that she would like done, the wwoofer told her that he would rather she told him no more than two jobs at once, for he could not remember anymore than that. When he had finished his jobs each day, the eager host would rush around giving him long lists of other things that she would like doing, it made little sense really, for the list just got longer and longer and more confusing. Adam mentioned it to the fellow carpenter who was working on the Gypsy wagon, and he sympathised with the volunteer and said:

"That is what she is like, I get it all the time!"

The working wanderer could not tell his host what his problem was, because he did not know exactly, but only that he could not understand more than a few words of simple instruction at the time. Usually this worked out just fine, but in this case, no amount of requests from Adam made the slightest bit of difference. He had tried to get tried to get to the root of the problem with help from doctors, but to no avail.

Information also came in the guise of objects, the trees, plants, tools and equipment his host showed him, they would also have to be understood. They were not complicated instructions, for example one may be:

"Take the saw hanging up in the shed and cut this branch

off for me please," his host may ask.

Two things struck Adam about this simple instruction, firstly, he could assimilate information about objects which were not man made, easier than he could things that were. Nature had a natural order to it, and the objects in it seemed to be less disruptive to the eye. Adam could assimilate these far easier than he could objects which man had designed, for example, looking at tools in a shed, which would just be a blur to him. Both types of information would still take the wwoofer considerable amounts of time to understand, particular if there were more than two commands, but on the whole, volunteering on farms was much simpler than being in urban areas, where Adam was overwhelmed with information which his brain would not compute. He realised that there were many people like this, who did not enjoy being amidst the rush and speed of modern day life, but he would carry on being close to the land and the peace which it offered.

From Sussex, the nomadic farmer moved across to Dorset and helped round up sheep and cattle for a few weeks. Soon, his fear of beasts, such as bulls and mad cows began to dissipate, as he became familiar with techniques to overcome it. He realised that often the animals were as frightened as he was, and that their main concern was whether or not you were bringing them food or you wanted to make them into food. If a bull was not threatening him as he fed them, he was calm. He had also learnt that if a bull was threatening him he must still stay calm, but could then jump up and frighten a charging attacker. Bulls knew then not to challenge the unpredictable helper...most of the time.

It was common for volunteers in the wwoof movement to

stay for just a few weeks and then move on to another place, though sometimes they may stay for a far shorter period or far longer, for months or even years. It all depended on what had to be done, with regard to both the wwoofers plans and the host's. In time, Adam too would find a particular region that he was very fond of and have the joy of settling for a while in one place.

Dorset was beautiful and Adam moved on to another farm, where the main help needed was in the woodlands with a small team of people. The farm was just a small part of the enormous estate that was owned by a *Sir* somebody. Adam stayed in a stable that had been converted into a cosy little dwelling and got straight into the tasks at hand, with the other land workers.

The sun cut into the forest as they walked through the delight of December. 'They' were three. One wwoofer and two foresters, heading for an area they would tidy for the day. As they walked, frost under foot, they spoke of trees. Pausing by a Yew tree, one told of his love of making longbows, an astounding ability to make such ancient weapons with skills nearly lost. He would bring in his War Bow the following day and all would marvel at it and the whooshing sound as the arrow was released. Yet for now, they worked, using only hand tools to cut back an overgrown part of the woods. It was soothing to be in nature again and the nomad was in his element. Working quietly, far from the noise of busy roads and modern places. The calm of the activities soaked right through Adam's hungry soul, as he worked away until his heart was content. A fire stood in a clearing which they had made, and they all watched it silently, one of earth's great attention keepers, the wanderer was thrilled by such natural wonders.

As he was placing leaves that he had collected onto a compost pile, he saw that an acorn had begun sprouting in the warmth of the decomposing process. He had never seen such a thing, and he marveled at the beautiful small seed of a tree that he held in his hand.

One day, this may be a grand old oak tree, he thinks to himself

Nature is incredible, I cannot believe that such a thing can happen.

To him it was no different from alchemy, this tiny piece of matter that could have easily just dissolved into the ground and disappeared. Yet when the conditions were right, the energy it stored within had sprouted out and with proper nurturing, the seedling would flourish. He asked the woodsman if he could have the small life that he held and he agreed, happy that he saw the magnificence of the simple thing, as they too loved the wonders of the woods. He took the acorn back with him to his room and planted it in a very small pot, watering it and watching it grow, little by little.

When it is time to move onto the next venue in Dorset, Adam hops on a bus, with his backpack containing the oak seedling and makes his way down to the community where he will stay. Like the first place he ever stayed at Brazil, this too offers courses of a spiritual nature. It is because nature is spiritual that they also give workshops on the more practical matters of life and the land. They have one on making a sewage water filtration system from reeds.

Another on repairing garden tools and another on Hazel Wood Coppicing.

It is in the grounds of the big old house that Adam helps, tending the garden and preparing it for the depths of the winter to come, clearing the land and enjoying the clear bright days that light up the ice that is all about them. There are many people living in the community and the wandering land worker enjoys there company, until he begins to fall ill. Adam develops full-blown influenza. In his delirious state, he has forgotten about the homeopathic remedies which he has previously taken for such serious ailments, but instead he receives the soothing company of a lady that he has met in the community. She visits him, checking his fire and making the shivering patient hot drinks. She seems immune to his flu, until a few days later she too begins to ache, but the strong girl just carries on tending the land and soon her symptoms go away. Adam tries, but it seems to have hit him differently, this is not a case of 'man flu', but we all have different constitutions and varying immune systems.

It is immensely painful to even stand up, he feels completely hammered all over and so he resigns himself to just receiving the unconditional help that this lovely soul administers to him. This is the force of nature, a virus so powerful that it can overtake one's own desire to move. Not even the nomad can go anywhere now. He is lucky to have such an earthy girl to help him and he thanks her by giving her a gift. He tells her the story of how he discovered the acorn and what a wonderful thing it seemed to him. Adam then gives her the small seedling, which he has carefully carried from his last host's estate.

One week later he is up and about and back to his duties

in the community. Once again, the nomad lives with the bliss and simplicity of open fires, chopping wood and being amongst like-minded souls. Though two of the community members are a little bit too like-minded as they also like the lady that Adam is beginning to form a relationship with. Only, she does not want to be with them and is fond of the nomad. They snatch the odd moment they have off from work to roam in the countryside and be away from the jealous men. It will not be long before the wanderer makes his way to his Christmas placement, a woodland farm in Devon where he has organized to stay.

2

The nomad bids his lady friend goodbye for now and takes a train to Devon. He buys a return ticket, as it is only a few shillings more than a one way.

Strange though, he thinks, for he has no plans to come back this day.

Yet on the way, he does not get such a good feeling about his next farm host in Devon, but not sure why, he continues, hiking the last five miles through country roads to get there.

As he arrives, the place looks deserted, there should be at least a few people about, according to the details that he has received, but there is no one there to greet him. Later, he will discover that they had forgotten that Adam was coming. He is not sure what to do now, Christmas is not a time to be out alone. Perhaps he could return to Sussex and stay at his old flat, but instead he decides to ring the community that he has just come from.

After explaining what has happened, they welcome him back to stay with them for Christmas and the lonesome wanderer is relieved to have company at this time. He makes his way back and settles back in.

It is in a morning meeting the following day that the gentle soul receives an unpleasant shock. One of the men, who has a liking for the lady Adam has met, becomes outrageously rude. He is so annoyed that his territory is threatened, that he throws insult after insult at the keen volunteer and because this man is a community member, that has expressed a desire for Adam not to stay this Christmas, the nomad has forty eight hours to leave. The group had agreed that they would not receive volunteers or even guests in their Bed and Breakfast over the Christmas period and though all but he and the other lady fancier are the only two who object to Adam presence, the group must stay with the decision that they have agreed upon. It is a shocking state of affairs and one that several others of the members are appalled at too, as they are only too pleased to have the company of the friendly wwoofer over the Christmas season. He finds himself somewhat distraught at the man's vicious attack and consoles himself with the best friend he has, nature, doing what has to be done. Wandering through the country lanes, he makes his plea to the Oneness.

Dear Oneness,
I find myself in a bit of a predicament, would you please guide me to where I should be?

Adam has put all mystical matters aside, but at times like this, he must use the tools he has to improve his situation. Few would believe the events that follow, they are certainly going to appear in his nomads notes soon. A particular farm came to mind that Adam had read much about, a small holding that had a legendary reputation and was not far away. Several times, Adam had tried to arrange a time to stay and help there, but it had not come about. He knew that it was but a stones throw from where he walked right now, and decided to take a chance by paying them a visit, they sounded like a friendly bunch of young organic farmers. It was worth a go, perhaps they would be in need of some help. Besides, his intuition seemed to be pulling him there.

Ice underfoot and weight in his heart, he followed the country paths of Dorset until he came to the place – not knowing what to expect. As he arrived he was greeted by the scene of a team of people preparing a cider press and the warm call of "hellos" and "come in". He explained what had happened and that he was looking for a place to wwoof over Christmas. It transpired that the farmers had hoped to go away, but had not managed to arrange a 'house and farm sitter' so one of them may have to stay behind to tend to the many animals.

"Yes, I remember speaking to you on the phone Adam, thank you for coming over to visit us. Look, it might be a bit of a lonely time for you here on your own, but you are welcome to stay and look after the animals if you like. There are loads of pigs that need feeding! Then I can go away with my family for a few days. What do you think?"

Having had quite a bit of wwoofing experience in dozens of places, he jumped at the chance to look after what he could see was a beautifully kept little farm. He could move in to a caravan that they had immediately, and although temperatures were around freezing, it had a decent wood burning stove to keep him warm. Adam would have a few days training on the essential needs of the Jersey cows, pigs, chickens, geese, ducks, dogs and cats, then the family would go off for Christmas to see their parents. It was a wonderful opportunity, the farm was absolutely idyllic.

In the end, it would not be such a lonely time, for Adam's female companion would come and visit him often. There would also be other visitors who came to lend a hand with milking the few cows that they had. They too stayed, sharing the rich and tasty pheasant stew that they had brought with them. Yet each morning, the task of feeding the pigs was down to Adam. They were beautiful animals, not just common pinks but spotted and shaded ones too, with browns and blacks along their backs. They seemed to be incredibly intelligent animals, the nomad would need to be on his toes. Some were big, the males especially could be particularly intimidating, if one allowed them to be so.

It was a thrilling time for Adam, he could not want for more, so close to the type of environment that he had been born into himself. Yet with every beginning comes an end and this situation was no different. The wandering pig sitter heard news from the community up the road, that the insulting man who stayed there had been asked to leave, he was no longer welcome at the place. Justice had found its way of rising. He was still friends with the lovely lady he met, and from time to time they would go out on an excursion into the big wide world. Romance would blossom for a time, but it would not continue. One cannot make things grow in life that are not meant to.

When the owners of the farm from heaven return, they invite Adam to stay on longer. He goes to the local market with them, selling the produce from their farm and attends social gatherings that they host in their rather splendid barn. It is staged on two floors and the sheer volume of guests and cider soon raise the temperature of the place. This is truly a phenomenal Wwoof venue, the depiction of the ideal opportunities available on organic farms around the world. Adam has come to love this way of life and all that it offers. This particular farm is hugely popular and the nomad reminds himself that when he writes down his nomad notes, which he will not name the farm, for they already receive hundreds of requests from people who would like to volunteer there. He has hopes of publishing his thoughts on helping on farms, and would not like to burden this venue with many more enquiries, for they would never get any work done in this case.

Adam had already started to make a few friends in the area, one had a farm of his own just a half a mile away. He too had many pigs who roam freely and invited Adam to come and help on his spread of land. There was a simple place to stay on the land, it looked like a gypsy wagon, but was actually a shepherd's hut. It would turn out to be the farm volunteer's most memorable wwoof accommodation, a tiny wooden home perched upon an old trailer. Steps led up to its creaking door, with ample gaps in it to ventilate the wood smoke. It had been made by the farmer, not having a house on his land, he had lived in it for a time, before upgrading to a monster of an antique caravan, that was equally attractive. A bent old chimney took the smoke away from this romantic but practical dwelling, set amidst fields – where pigs wandered nearby. Water was from a hose pipe outside, unless it was frozen up, for the depths of winter had set in.

The toilet was of the kind that Adam had seen many times before as he travelled far a field. All of the farms in France, Portugal, Spain and Hungary which he had stayed on used this compost type depository. A tall timber room with a section below to collect the essential fall, the throne usually having unrivalled views of nature. Often mixed with ash, soil or straw, but in this case there was ample saw dust to cover the daily needs. Utterly hygienic, a system that allowed its waste to decompose in a short period of time. It was a peaceful place to be, looking out over the field of hungry pigs from a frosty seat.

Having been in the area for some time, Adam got to know a few more local people. One asked him if he would restore an old wooden bench that she had and the carpenter at heart was only too pleased to complete the work, once his daily volunteering was completed, happy to add a few gold coins to his purse, for it was running low. The farm host did not mind either, even lending tools and giving some materials. When the job was done, the lady then asked him to make some things for her out of wood, and before long, Adam had enough money to consider fulfilling his plan. For he had wanted to Wwoof from Sussex to Scotland, but such dreams still need funding, even if his lifestyle had little financial outlay involved. He wanted to experience as many different farms as he could and acquire a varied range of skills. Though for the time being, there were other adventures to be had where he was, until a natural gap appeared again and of course it always did.

The freezing water pipes presented a few problems with regard to getting the pigs the water they needed and when it came, they would make the most of it. Adam had left it running to fill their troughs whilst he fed the chickens that roosted nearby. When he finished, he turned around and saw that the trough were full, but one of the brighter pigs was dragging the hose in his mouth, over toward an large dip in the ground, that formed a pond during wetter times. When the smart swine reached the area, he dropped the hose in to let it fill. The nomad did not have the heart to turn the water off until it had filled, by which time, several of the pig's friends had arrived to splash about in the icy water. Adam's father had often told him just how incredible these animals were, now he was seeing it for himself first hand.

A little gas cooker gave a hint of luxury in the hut where Adam stayed. Normally, he would eat in one end of the barn that was the other side of the farm. A room had been built in it, with a powerful wood burning stove, this is where visitors gathered and food was to be found. At lunch time Adam would eat simple meals of pork and bread, sometimes cheese. The evenings would see a wide array of winter vegetables that were grown on the farm, often in poly-tunnels, but the most attractive part of the nomad's diet was the endless barrels of home made cider that stood under the eaves at one end of the barn. When the wwoofer tired of such simple life, he wandered to see his friends, who he had made at the Christmas farm. Even when he visited them, he helped them, making sausages and sharing a bite to eat with them. It was a pleasure to do so and the way of things in this part of the world, not so far from Sussex.

Life was so different from that which Adam had known in the summer months in Sussex, such modern things as internet and television he rarely saw on his farming travels. He was so tired from the days physical work, in the elements and air, that sleep was long and deep, broken only by the call of the empty wood burning stove in the shepherd's hut, at which he would rise in the night to feed it. There was always something to feed on the farms, even the small bird that would come through a gap in the roof of the shepherd's hut, he too was after a morsel of food. His visits became more frequent when snow began to fall. Most people would not like a bird flying into visit them in their house, but Adam's situation was rather becoming to the visitor.

In time, the nomad was becoming more and more a part of the land. His hair had got wild and curly again, as too had his beard, he was at one in the natural environment, until relentless snow storms battled. Initially, there was no problem with the snow, the wwoofer was warm, fed and occupied, but when the drifts stopped all of the other activities on the farm, the place became a difficult one to manage in. Everyone in England was suffering, it was January 2009, the snow was so thick that the country was coming to a stand-still. The army were called in to many parts, to clear the roads, people were getting stuck all over the place, stranded in the freezing conditions. Yet some of the main roads were still passable, one of which was only two miles from where Adam sat. He made a decision to return to the flat if there was still a space available for him there. A phone was the limit of the farms technology, and Adam made full use of it by contacting his friend who owned the seafront abode, the wanderer had done without a mobile phone up until now.

To Adam's delight the flat was free. The ground had been rock solid where he was and not much work could be done amidst the blizzards that covered it, and so the farmer did not mind him leaving. He looked forward to the comfort of brick walls again and the luxury of being able to turn on heat by the flick of a switch. To have tap water twenty four hours a day. The central heating lacked the wonderful whiff of smoldering logs, but the wanderer was ready to forego that pleasure and replace it with the ease of which his abode could be heated. A few days back in civilization would be good, he would have a chance to confirm some more wwoofing placements on other farms, hopefully working his way all the way up to Scotland.

The snow was still thick, but Adam felt that it was a good day to hitch-hike from Dorset back to Sussex, as he was far more likely to get a ride on a day like this than any other. People did not often stop for hitch-hikers in England any more, they were too frightened that they would get attacked and sometimes they were. Whoever picked him up today would be brave enough to be out in the fraught conditions and tough enough to deal with anyone thumbing a lift that got out of hand. Adam stuck out his hand and looked like someone who really needed a ride. A sensible looking chap, even with his slightly wild look, but to the trained eye, he was clearly a man of the land.

To his delight, he did not have to wait long on this snowy day, it was a young man in a van that offered the ride, as he pulled into the lay by where Adam stood. They got on well and talked about travel and the wild. Adam noticed that the driver was wearing a *National Trust* t-shirt, this was a warden who worked for the countryside management organisation. Adam was right, this was a man of the land and he had spotted the nomad as being one too. He would have to get four more rides and walk an awful long way before getting back to Sussex, it would turn out to be a terribly long day in the snow, however, he would make it safely. It would be a good day to hitch-hike and the journey would be free, all except for the lunch he would buy his current driver, for the nomad was so pleased with the news that he was about to find out.

"How do you get to wear one of those then?" Adam

asked, remarking on the drivers proudly worn emblemed t-shirt. Perhaps it would be his destiny to become a warden.

He found out that he could volunteer for the group and that they were actually looking for an assistant warden in Devon quite soon. This was an incredibly rare opportunity, many people longed to be a warden for the National Trust. It would not be a post that he would stay at long, for he was not cut out to be a warden. Yet it would be a phenomenal experience, one that he had to have in order to know that it was not for him.

"Do you mean I will get to drive one of those lovely green Land Rovers too?" Adam asked, sure enough, he would. A week later, he would attend an interview and secure a position. It would not start until May, but that would be fine, he would have time to carry on wwoofing for a while, before making his way all the way back down to Devon to volunteer in a green Land Rover. It would be another experience and another string to his bow.

Back in Sussex, Adam arranged another couple of farms to volunteer at, that would be enough to get him on his way. There were infinite possibilities to learn about matters of the land and all that lived and grew on it naturally. There was no need to pay out vast sums of money for courses if one had enough time to go and wwoof. Adam learnt that he was born during the same year in which the movement started, 1971. Initially it had been called *'Weekend Workers on Organic Farms'* and was aimed to help people who just wanted to get out into the big green to help for a couple of days. It grew so widely, that in time, helpers could go to nearly one hundred countries around the world, experiencing a cultural exchange, whilst volunteering just four to six hours a day. The group interested Adam hugely and he began writing down all of the practical things that one would need to know in order to go and wwoof. There did not seem to be one central organisation that ran the wwoofing in every country. He alone had wwoofed in five already, since he began his journeys nearly ten years before and he was about to add another two to the list as he worked his way up England, onto Wales and Scotland. When he did some internet searching, he found that there was not a book on the subject and thought perhaps he would write one. He discovered that each country ran themselves autonomously and realised that it would be impractical to contact each one to ask if they objected in any way to him writing the book. He also decided that he would not look at any of the guidelines to wwoofing that appeared on websites, but instead devise a list that he found had been useful to him. Ultimately, it would turn out to be very similar, yet it was spiced with humour and tales of his own experiences whilst he had wwoofed and worked his way around the world. Adam did not know it yet, but he would meet the founder of Wwoof and present her with his dinky little pocket book. She would be very pleased with it and it would go on to sell in many countries around the world. It would also bring Adam to new frontiers, as he would have to embrace the tools of the modern age, such as computers in order to produce it. The few shekels he may earn from the sales could help him to have other land based adventures.

Adam is drawn to help on a farm that works with *Horse Whispering*. It has always been a dream of his to buy a horse in foreign lands and ride through wild places. It may not be a dream that he chooses to make a reality in this lifetime, but he is still keen to be close to the gentle art of

Whispering and makes his way up to the farm in Wiltshire.

When he meets the man who will show him this way of communicating, it is no surprise that he has a peaceful demeanour and is quiet, confident and serene. They walk together, slowly to the horses and the man stops some distance from them. A stallion comes over and nuzzles him. Adam is a little apprehensive around animals he does not know, but wisely so, but he is soon at ease in the presence of this beautiful horse, watching the Whisperer, looking at his energy, which he sees visibly radiating. It is clear that the horse also feels his peace. Movements in each of the communicator's body language are subtle, but the slightest change can reveal much to the eye that sees intention – and Adam's is becoming finely tuned.

He is invited to stand next to the Whisperer and Adam learns by 'direct transmission', a technique he remembers first seeing from a martial arts teacher in Spain. The teacher consciously transmits physical energy in a non-physical way. Thought to thought, mind to mind, only in this situation, the whisperer is doing this with the horse, not only sending his own intention, but also listening and reading the horses. It is a powerful tool for the receptive, who may sense the intention of the next action or movement. This is very useful in martial arts, but also to the horse whisperer. Animals are already well developed in what is not an art for them, but more of a sixth sense, an in-built natural ability. A student witnessing such events may absorb knowledge rapidly and become extremely sensitive to all that is happening before his or her eyes.

The highly interested wandering wwoofer is permitted to go inside the enclosure with the horse. They approach each other slowly, smelling, looking and watching. When the horse tries to win the partnership and be ruler over Adam, he submits at first to the animal's grandeur and looses his footing. The Whisperer encourages him to make back his ground and be in control of the horse, letting him know that the human is chief. It is an unnatural state of affairs that only came about when man took ownership of such beauties, but as that is the reality here, Adam expresses a dominant position, and leadership. In no time at all, he has the respect of the beast.

He may never learn all of the simple rules and ways of Whispering, for it is not his path, yet what he has seen will have a knock-on effect with his understanding of man's relationship with other living things. Whether a boy who bullies viciously or a person who speaks to him maliciously – the rules are very similar. Energy will affect us if we give it the chance to do so, it will get into us. In the case of the horse, it will not last long. For an owner, it can last a lifetime, if one develops uncomfortability around the animal. It is of course a natural law. The threatened must rise and show that they will not be beaten, rise to a place of seniority. In time, one may find that we do not need to fold to the feeling of fear, of being beaten or the insecurity of not knowing another person. It has taken Adam a long time to overcome his own fear of being hurt, after his head has struck the ground several times in bicycle accidents and fists have also knocked him out.

Man has brought animals out of the wild and tamed them for his own use. In doing so, we no longer have many beasts roaming our lands and have ruled out potential threats around us as humans have evolved. Though naturally, large animals still have their primitive senses and finely tuned perceptions, as perhaps humans do if we dig deeply enough within ourselves. It would be a while before Adam would be tested by life to the full, to see how much he has learnt about these things, and in time he would face a potentially deadly challenge. His life will depend on drawing upon his knowledge, but not this day.

For now, he will face another test. On leaving the horse whispering farm, he moves onto to his next placement on the Welsh English Borders. As is the law of averages, not all we meet will be compatible with our own psyches. We can keep quiet and bear it, or if possible, remove ourselves from that which does not fit with us. In this case, Adam chooses to do the latter, as he is not suited to the unpleasant temperament of the owner of the next farm and is unhappy there. Subtly, he tells the owner that he will not be staying. Yet his next place is a week off, he must find somewhere to sleep in the meantime. Though he has his train tickets to get to most of his other hosts, Adam has less than £50 and no other savings, he still has no credit or cash point card anymore, or even a bank account, since becoming a pilgrim of the road on leaving Wales. The days are bright, but the nights are icy and he relishes the thought of a challenge.

The hardy traveller makes a shelter in a thick woodland for the night. The going is tough, and he is tried to his limits, as he feels like a homeless wanderer, but a fire soon warms his spirit and spurs him on through the night. What is more, he is gradually ticking off all of the things which he wishes to do in life...and to be able to sleep wild in an English forest in winter is another.

When daylight comes, it is with bright sunshine again, and though it is still freezing, the wanderer is happy to be free, glad that he did not stay on at his previous place.

Toward lunch time, he reaches a pub and goes in for a pint of their finest ale and a jacket potato. He has a plan, for he now travels with an old mobile phone that he has been given and what is more, he has credit on it. The beauty of the wwoof world offers the solution, for he calls some farms to see if they are in need of any immediate help for a few days. The first two phone calls brings no reply, the third an answer machine, the fourth a "not at the moment thanks", but the fifth brings a 'yes' and he is off again, hitch-hiking up to North Wales.

It is a tiring business travelling in this way and the nomad is relieved to reach the security of a farm again. A small place, but the hearts of the owners are big. They welcome him warmly and show him to the caravan where he will stay. There is a heater in there, but thankfully the weather has made a turn for the better, and things are starting to warm up a little.

In return for the hospitality they offer, Adam does what ever tasks need doing. They mostly grow vegetables in the two poly-tunnels, so the wwoofer helps to weed them through. Though by the grace of wwoofers luck, they also keep a few horses, and the helper is able to get involved with feeding them and cleaning up all the leather tack that they wear, building his confidence around the fine animals. The host's two children are also happy to have some company, and Adam enjoys playing football with them, in the ample stretch of grassland that they have made their pitch upon. It is not a bad way of life to have, for the nomad or the children, and he remembers his days on the small farm which his own parents once had.

In some ways he was reliving his youth, but in others, he

was doing something that he could not have done then, at such a young age. Now he was learning new skills, for the road ahead would take him far a field again, even abroad, and it was important that he was comfortable with being out in the wild. Though for now, he prepared to move on from this very short stay and continue his wwoofing journey in England, up toward the *Lake District* of *Cumbria*.

3

The variety of places that Adam had stayed at over the years was enormous, this time his bed would be in a bunk house, accommodation used for groups that visited the Lake District and stayed on the farm. It was a wooden building, probably constructed in the 1920s, and was big enough to house a dozen or so people, but he was the only visitor at this time. A couple with their two children ran the farm, a six hundred acre place that stretched way up into the crags that the farms sheep roamed upon. It would be Adam's job to go up into the mountains with sheep dogs to bring down the vast flocks of sheep for their immunisations.

On the second day, after the wandering wwoofer had been shown around the lie of the land on the back of a quad bike, he went up to the fells with a few farmers to round up the sheep. Adam's job was to cut them off before the scitty animals made for their escape. It was not the first time the wwoofer had done this, on a farm in Dorset he had had to round up *Hebridean* sheep, whilst they tried to jump over the top of him. This breed were slightly more subdued, but it was the boggy wetlands that he had to cross which proved to be the most difficult work, running miles from rock to rock, as he tried to head off the sheep and send them back down to the farmers. It was exhausting work and took all day, but the nomad enjoyed the challenge immensely.

All the sheep were brought down safely and the next day, the farm help learned how to carefully turn them onto their backs whilst they had jabs for all sorts of pesky mites.

Although it was not the right time of year to shear the sheep, Adam also learnt that it cost more to do the job, than the farmer was getting back for the sale of the wool, in some cases it was barely worth selling.

How did farming come to this terrible state of affairs? He wondered.

There were also horses at the place and the nomad's fondness of the animals got him the job of feeding them, along with bringing in the chickens at night and digging over the vegetable patch. These were years that the wanderer could simply never forget, the tiring physical days and the early nights, often with a pencil scribbling away, adding to his nomad notes.

When Adam went out way into the depths of the fells with the farmer and his truck, he learnt that he was only a few miles away from his next host, who was also in the magnificent Lake District. The next time they went, the nomad took his back pack too, and dropped it off at the farm. He was not due at the place for a few days, but decided that he would walk across the mountains to get there, as it was only about twelve miles away and would be much easier without his pack. Sometimes the wanderer was exceptionally well developed in matters of the land, other times he did not seem to grasp basic principles at all. For although his next wwoof host was only that distance away, twelve mountain miles can be like a twenty five mile level road walk. Nevertheless, when it was time to head on over to his penultimate farm on this tour, he went on foot. Once over the peak that separated him from Lake Coniston and the next farm, he popped on a bus for the last leg of the journey, arriving at the breathtaking watermill where he would volunteer for the next week. Although the wheel was not running, it was still a staggering sight to behold, because of its height and sheer size.

His next placement must have been the quintessential organic farm. A river running through it, the hosts with volumes upon volumes of knowledge stored in their minds and hearts and an exceptionally well organised schedule for its wwoofers. There were two this time, Adam and Caroline. She was from London and would partner him in his tasks through the week. Henry, the owner, turned out to be a director of the Wwoof U.K organisation. It was a complete surprise to the wanderer when he spoke about his plans to write a simple A-Z book for wwoofers. Henry then told him about his own connection, which he held in a voluntary capacity. He loved the idea of a practical book about wwoofing, and when Adam had finished writing it the following autumn, he sent one along to the friendly host.

The mill itself was full of antiques and bicycles, which Adam found to be incredibly interesting. There were cycles from every decade and perhaps an antique for each one over the last five hundred years too. It was like walking into a fairytale for the nomad, he loved all of these things, particularly as he was often able to admire them whilst he broke off from making kindling wood next door. As with many of the farms, the home cooked food was delicious and these particular meals were cooked in the *Rayburn* oven that Adam so often split kindling for.

Working with wood was a favourite activity for this host, during the week they made a combination between a gate and hurdle from green timber, and Adam thought perhaps that it should be called a 'Gurdle.' He was becoming increasingly interested in words, as he spent more and more of his free time writing. It had been a joy to tour some of the farms on England's green and pleasant land. People would often ask him in the future, what his favourite country was that he had been to, and his answer would be *England*. Though soon, he would head off to Scotland, for his final farm stay this year. The adventurous walker decided not to try and walk to it, although it was wholly achievable, he had already secured a discount rail ticket to *Dumfries*. From there, he would hitch-hike to the place where he would stay.

He reaches the Scottish farm safely, after exchanging stories with yet another driver who picked him up. This man tells the hitch-hiker all about the woman who he is separated from, who now lives in the middle of France and how he drives over to see her in the truck that Adam is in now. It is a 1970s Land Rover, the ride is as rough as the surface of the moon and the hiker is glad that he is not travelling that far with the gentleman. It is a strange phenomenon, getting into vehicle with somebody you do not know, likewise, a vehicle stopping for somebody they have not met before. You are suddenly a part of each others lives and the unsaid deal of chatting openly is nearly always done before the driver even pulls over to pick you up. Then as quickly as it began, the relationship is over.

His new hosts leave most days to go and run a shop in the next town. It is a grey and lonely farm which Adam finds himself on, but when he has finished his tasks, he spends time drafting the book that he would like to publish.

The nomad has now volunteered on organic farms in England, Scotland, Wales, France, Portugal, Spain and Hungary. Doing other voluntary work in Brazil, Latvia and India too. His concise words describe how one may go about such a thing, written in a brief and clear fashion. The same year, he will publish it and it will steadily sell a small number of copies worldwide. He can see this happening and the goal keeps him feeling bright whilst he works mostly alone on this damp and windy placement in Scotland.

The wandering wwoofer does make a few friends at the farm, they are baby goats whose mother has died. His job is to hand rear the kids by feeding them with milk from another goat. Each morning he takes out the five bottles of milk, which have been warmed again to a mother's body temperature and tries to get the sweet little monsters to suckle. They always take the feed, but not always straight away. It is a wonderful job to be given and Adam willingly attends to the babies most days.

Sometimes the job is followed by one of feeding some bulls too. They are young, but still well able to cause injury if one gets on the wrong side of them. Adam makes sure he stays on the right side of them. They are a good natured bunch and soon get used to the idea that he is a bringer of food and so they do not bother him. The wanderers confidence in dealing with animals has risen dramatically since he began wwoofing, in turn, the practice has helped him become as focused on earthly matters as he had previously on that of the esoteric. For a time he will sway nearer to being in the body than he will to that of looking into the unseen energies of life, that have previously been of such great interest to him. It is a leaning that he will ignore for a while, until he learns how to balance the two.

When the farm trainee is not feeding animals, he is digging trenches again, but this time not for electric cables, as he did in Sussex, but for potatoes. The farmer's wife has some days off and shows Adam a simple technique for increasing yield for the crop. As it grows, each time the plant appears above ground level, one can recover it with fresh soil. This way, the plant stem sprouts out again and these arms will also eventually grow potatoes. The procedure can be repeated a few more times until by cropping season, the trench is full of the goodies. These types of facts thrill Adam, he is so interested in the simple things in life, the ones that sustain the basic human needs. It makes him wonder about life and sustainability.

How is it that a child can know how to reprogram a computer or download things from the internet, but not know how to grow a potato?

It will soon be time to go to Devon so that Adam can take up his voluntary position with the National Trust as a *Countryside Warden*. He makes his way from Scotland, back down to Sussex, where he has secured a few weeks building work. Staying in the flat again, overwhelmed with the comfort he finds there. The place smells unlived in, it is not often used and in the short time that he is there, he gives it a thorough airing. He also has the joy of seeing some of his old friends again, although in the years that he has been away, he has lost contact with many. It is spring 2009, the road has been long since Adam left for his wild adventures at the turn of the millennium. His brothers and sister, mother and father all live nearby and when he calls on them, they are pleased to see that he is happy, though it is not long before they bid him farewell again as he leaves for Devon.

The money he has earned doing building work, repairing the outside of a house, will be very useful in the coming weeks, for the new position with the National Trust is unpaid. As with wwoofing, Adam will receive accommodation, however, he will not receive any food or money toward it, he must find his own way of providing this. He worries not about the arrangements and instead focuses his attention on getting down to Devon. Buying an old bicycle, he fills it back and front with things he will need for his stay in the countryside. Hopping on a train with it, he makes his way on yet another adventure, open to all that it may bring. Strapped to its side is an air rifle, he is prepared for the possibility of leaner times ahead.

The cottage he stays in is wonderful, a gorgeous old place in a quiet sleepy village.

"It should be a bit livelier when the other volunteers turn up," his new boss tells him, but what Adam does not know is that they will never come whilst he stays there, for his boss has not arranged any yet. Nevertheless, there will be ample to interest the new land worker, there are paths to strim, paths to strim and paths to strim! The absence of other volunteers means that Adam must do most of the work. Whilst he does it around the wild places backing onto the village, he notices that many tourists visit this quaint little place. It seems that there is nowhere to empty their purse into, or buy mementos of their country day out. Adam's funds are becoming low, soon he will not be able to eat and he takes a chance by investing his last shekels in something that he thinks will make him some money.

Flour, he will make rustic bread to sell to the visitors. There is water in his tap and Adam knows how precious it is to have such wonders. He had once learnt how to mix it with flour to cultivate a natural yeast, known as Sourdough, that is ready within a few days. By regularly adding to it, the yeast may continue to be good for years and years.

A warm spring is upon them and Adam decides that he will turn his hand to making Rye bread and bakes many batches of it. Early each morning before work, he bakes the loaves that he has prepared the night before, places them in a basket outside the cottage and sits it on a table, covering them with a cloth. He places an 'honesty money box' beside his sign that reads:

Rye Bread for Sale

Each night he brings in the basket, which is usually empty, and with it the money box. In this way, he has just enough cash to live on.

The weather is hotting up and so he makes a simple lemonade and sells that too. He is pleased that his small venture works and through it makes many friends amongst the villagers, who also buy his goods, as well as the tourists. In the garden that comes with the cottage, he plants potatoes and other fruit and vegetables, using the techniques that he has learnt over the years. Around the paths that are his job to clear, wild garlic thrives, so Adam cleans it and puts it in jars with olive oil, this too he sells outside the cottage. Strictly speaking, he is not permitted to sell anything there, but all turn a blind eye to the wanderer who is making his way in such a resourceful fashion, even his boss kindly looks the other way. He could be claiming *Unemployment Benefit*, as volunteers are allowed to, but he is not. Somehow, the nomad always gets by. In the summer, he will go to the beach, which is not too far away and catch some of the many Mackerel fish that swim just off the shore. Cooking them on the stones as he did with the fish he caught in India and remembering much about his travels as he does so.

In his spare time, he works on the book he is writing about the wwoofing and volunteering he has done on his way. It is all done on paper, as the wanderer is a little behind the times with regard to technology, and he does not know how to prepare it on a computer. When the draft is finished, he sends it off to his sister in law, who will kindly type it all up for him so that he can go to the next stage of having it made into a book. Who knows, perhaps it will make a few pounds to help him on his way, for sometimes he does not have any money at all.

Things become tough when rainy weather sets in, as he cannot put out his goods for sale, but he must still eat. He is living on a shoestring and if he is not careful, he will have to eat his own laces. The rain goes on and his money runs out completely and for a couple of days he survives on wild garlic rye bread and lemonade, but man cannot live by bread alone, he must find something else to eat. As he looks out from the bathroom, onto the garden, he sees a rabbit hopping about. Adam picks up his gun, leans out of the window and shoots his dinner. He skins it and keeps the fur to make a lucky purse with, once it is dried and cured. Adding some spices to the meat and two cups of rice that he has left, that evening he enjoys a tasty meal. Though he does not like to kill, he has to eat and the nature of man rises up within all who hunger. He invites a friend for dinner, who brings a few red peppers that he has grown and they too go into the pot. When his visitor pulls out a bottle of wine, Adam is somewhat overwhelmed, when one has hungered and not fed, such delights are more appreciated and to the nomad, it is as if they are living like kings.

The lucky purse brings with it fine weather again and the rustic baker makes a basket of bread to put out. Soon he hears the sound of coins in his pocket, yet despite receiving not a penny from the National Trust to eat with, some people he works with complain to Adam about his selling of drinks and bread outside the home he lives in. It is not a house open to the public, but because it is owned by them, it is forbidden to sell a few loaves of bread on a table outside. They also complain about fish being barbecued on the stones of the beach, as the law forbids it, but even some of the local fisherman cook theirs there.

He can bear all of this and even the perfectly straight paths that he is asked to make through the countryside, though there is little natural about them. Yet when his boss asks him to make some small flags and go and put them in all the dogs mess on the paths to alert the dog's owners to the peril, Adam at first thinks he is joking, but no, he is serious. It is too much and after trying out the voluntary post for some months, the wanderer realises that he is not cut out to be a warden. Nevertheless, he has driven his green Land Rover and been given a good pair of leather boots, these alone will take him far, to many more places.

It is better to try and know that you do not want a thing, than to know that you have never tried but wish you had. Some of the locals are sorry to see his smiling face and light hearted ways vanish from their village, but he is gone...like a butterfly in the wind again, onto other shores.

4

Remarkably, the free spirit has a clean slate again, nothing binds him and he begins to consider new adventures. Will he ever tire of wandering? Perhaps. Though for now, he has a little time on his hands again and asks his friend who has the poorly house, if she would like him to do some more work on the property. It is a massive undertaking and the nomad come builder is glad that he did not try to tackle it all in one ago, alone. The master builder that he once worked with, erects scaffolding around the house so that he can finish another large wall. It is a lot of work as the home needs completely refacing, once all the old textured coating has first been scraped off. The owner has afforded another stage of the work to be completed, but the last section will have to wait until another time. Adam spends weeks on the house and is relieved to have completed this part of the job and painted it all.

It is time for a change for the wanderer, for he will wander no longer for a while. He has things to learn and jobs to do. Primarily to find out how to use computers. He decides to base himself in his home town for the summer of 2009, in order to carry out the task and rents a small room in a student house. They are away on leave and the arrangement suits him well, for the first time in years, he is independent and making his own way. Adam feels good about this and his raised self esteem helps him to focus on the task at hand, for he has much to learn about computers. He cannot attend a course in such matters, for he still suffers with a serious learning block, information simply just does not go in when taught in the traditional way, ever since he was smashed in the head, and perhaps even before. Sometimes a page on paper or on screen is just a complete blur to him and appears as a sold block of text. He is embarrassed by the condition and is only really coming to accept it now, at the age of thirty seven. He learns by asking the assistants at his local library, each time he gets stuck on some aspect of the infinitely complicated computers. They do not mind and in time he actually becomes friends with one or two of the librarians, who like to see his smiling face and naturally happy disposition. He is diligent in the course that he has set himself and every morning he is at the library just before it opens. The maximum time one can spend at the terminals is two hours, then one must leave the machines for an hour or so before one is permitted to return to them. This is ideal for the once wanderer, for he does his shopping or stretches his legs on the beach nearby.

As he learns, he goes through the document that his sister-in-law has typed up for him, the first draft of his wwoof book. It will take several hundred hours more to bring it up to the level it needs to be at, in order for it to be professional enough to sell as a paperback. Yet she has done him a great service in putting his words to paper and he agrees to pay her one day for the effort she has made. At present, he can only type about ten or so words per minute, but that is set to increase with all of the computer work he will do in the coming years.

Once the computer student has mastered the basics, he learns how to transfer the information he has prepared to an online book publisher. At first, the process seems to be quite complex, but in time, he is as comfortable with it as he is walking twenty miles in the countryside. It takes

Adam dozens and dozens of one to two hour sessions, using the library computers to reach this stage, it is a real struggle for the wanderer, the letters and numbers on the screen and keyboard are incredibly confusing and often he has to simply cut his session short because he cannot see straight or absorb the information in front of him. Somehow he battles through and eventually receives a copy by post of his little book on farm volunteering. It will take him five more attempts and the purchase of five more draft copies of the pocket book, before he is satisfied with the content enough to sell it the mainstream market. Before long, he makes it available for retail and it starts to sell at some of the most popular online stores. Not many copies, but enough to encourage the self-motivated student who has come far off the track of the wild to take part in some of the more modern ways of life.

He registers with the tax office again, this time his profession is 'author'. One huge difference has occurred within Adam's mind, he has no intention of closing the business this time, for it earns him a regular income. Besides, he will write more books as well. The profit is little, but sometimes little will be enough and all he needs in some parts of the world. In order to receive the money that he makes from his book, he opens a basic bank account, his credit rating will not allow any other kind. As far as the system is concerned, he does not exist anymore, since renouncing all he owned and becoming homeless. Naturally, the plastic money people have never written to him, they could not, for he has not had an address. The book carries a disclaimer that it may contain mistakes, as it is of an organic nature. In years to come, these copies will become quite rare as Adam will discover such delights as

'Spell Checking' tools in the future.

It is autumn and his pennies are low. The lady he sometimes works for can afford the next stage of the project to be done and he continues the work of restoring the outside of the house that he began the previous spring. The salt air of the coast it sits by has corroded the walls over the decades and he learns the skill of skimming, to bring a little more of the lovely home back to its former glory. He will not complete the project by the time harsher weather comes, as there is a lot more of the old textured coating to remove by hand first, but gradually the building is taking shape and it is an opportunity to earn a few more shekels to spur the nomad on to his next adventure.

"Nice job Adam, thank you. You are welcome to come back in the spring and do some more work on my house if you like." His boss says.

The more he has worked on the property, the more he likes the idea of home, perhaps one day he will have one or even a small piece of land of his own. He now knows enough about how to sustain himself on earth and would like to put his skills to good use. Yet winter is upon him and he does not relish the fact of being in the cold again this year and seeks milder climates. Not entirely sure of what direction to take, he considers what a place would have in order to attract him. A land where the sea would never be far away would suit him well, a sea warmed by the sun. So the wanderer decides that it should be an island that he visits for the winter months, one that knows some heat. The *Mediterranean* sounds like a place where these things could be possible, and so Adam heads for the clear blue waters of the *Greek* island of *Crete*.

Not all the people he knows give him their blessing on

his journey, for many wish that they could go themselves and wonder how it is that the nomad can live such a life. One thing is obvious, he has no fixed abode and has left the summer room that he had based himself in, stored the few boxes of possessions that he has with a friend and hit the road again. He may be free, but he is also homeless, but Adam knows this and also knows a practical truth, that it is not too difficult to be living outside in the wild, when it is warm and the countryside of rocky lands beckon.

The nomad sets off again, taking a one way flight to Crete, satisfied that the income he has created will see him through. It will not be enough to house him permanently, but coupled with the skills that he has developed to live in the wild and the money that he has saved from the building work, he aims to be gone for the entire winter. It is December and yet again, the wanderer leaves a dreary winter England and heads for the sun and so it is that Adam is on the road again, jotting in his journal.

He who wanders free may not know the comfort of regularity, but he is sure to meet incredible times ahead, times that will enrich his life forever. When we cease to be undaunted by the torrents of judgement and jealousy that rain upon us when the glow of an imminent journey flows from our being – we step into an entirely different world, an altered state of travel consciousness. A place from which we emanate untold potential joy.

Epilogue

It is winter 2009 and Adam leaves the freezing temperatures of England and touches down in the warmer air of *Heraklion*, in Northern Crete. Acclimatising in a delightful hostel in a smaller city, *Rethymno*, as he prepares for a long walk around the west coast of Crete. This is the sum total of his plan, walk in the wild. He sets off with pack on back, containing in the main all that he needs to survive.

It is a stunning land that he walks upon, with its red earth and kings of mountains that rise from the sea. The wanderer is blessed with warm and dry weather, as he follows the coastline, finding wild places in which to put his tent. Sometimes amongst trees, in a cave or on a beach. Walking between scents of thyme and sage, he is taken by this ancient place, where wild goats wander yonder. Adam is in awe at the simplicity in which he finds himself amongst again, it screams pure nature. On the roads he walks, only one car may pass an hour, as he looks out to the seemingly endless sea. The walker barely looks at a map, for when you are not going anywhere in particular, it is hard to become lost. He is just wandering, looking and breathing, keeping step with the company of the peace he feels.

The hungry man buys Feta cheese, olives and rustic bread, sometimes a local red wine or the kick of a strong Greek coffee. When he tires, he takes the more comfortable sleeping place of small hotels and eats more fruitfully. Yet not all is bright and rosy, it begins to rain hard on his wild walk, as he reaches the south west tip of Crete and strong winds drive the wet into his bones. It is still warm, but it would be wise to get undercover. The only shelter apart from his tent is a chapel perched upon a hill top, but when he comes to it, he finds that God is closed again and makes for the next town. He is out of drinking water, but one must not worry about these things when rain comes. Indents in rocky outcrops hold clear clean pools of the source of life that has just fallen into them and the thirsty nomad kneels down to lap up the fresh water naturally.

...*Continued in:*
'The Adventures of a Greenman'(Part 11):
Raw Travel Crete

The Adventures of a Greenman Series:

(in chronological order):

Part 1 Raw Beginning - *The First 30 Years of a Greenman*

Part 2 Raw Travel Brazil
Part 3 Raw Travel France
Part 4 Raw Travel Spain
Part 5 Raw Travel India
Part 6 Raw Travel New Zealand
Part 7 Raw Travel Wales
Part 8 Raw Travel Eastern Europe
  to 9
Part 10 Raw Travel England
Part 11 Raw Travel Crete
Part 12 Raw Travel Italy
Part 13 Raw Travel Europe (All European countries above)

Part 14 Raw Around the World Travel
    (Parts 2 - 12 of the series)

Part 15 I Travel Light:
    The Man Who Walked Out of the World.
    (Epic formed of parts 1-12 and new material)

Preview to follow!

According to **The Concise Oxford English Dictionary**, these are all definitions of *'raw'*:

"Not completely manufactured. Not analysed or corrected. Fresh to a thing".

(Very much like *'The Adventures of a Greenman'*).

I Travel Light
The Man Who Walked Out of the World

A novel style book, collating all of Adam's adventures since birth, and even a little before! All in one epic true story. Including parts 1 to 12 of:

'The Adventures of a Greenman Raw Travel Series'

...and some new material.

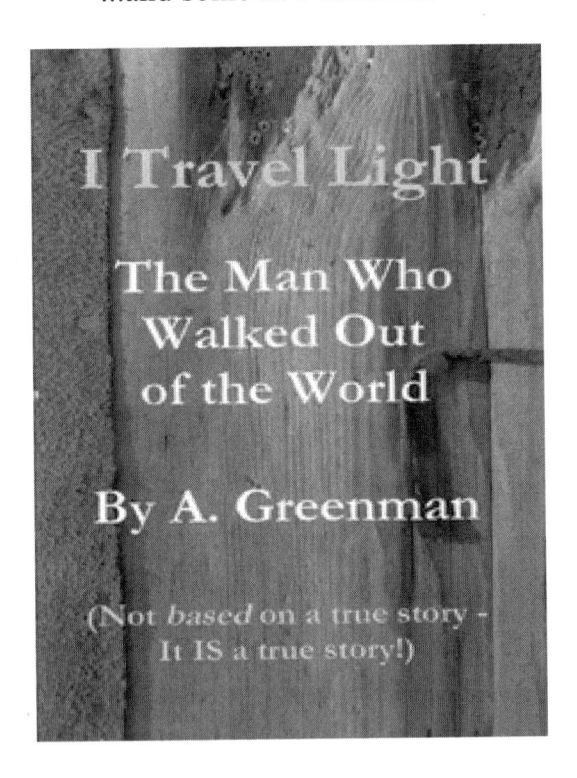

Praise for the novel
(From someone who really knows what is good for you!)
"When I had something important to do, I found myself reading this book instead - it is BRILLIANT!"

Dr. M. Longmore, author of the bestselling
'Oxford Handbook of Clinical Medicine'

Preview

I Travel Light
The Man Who Walked out of the World

Prologue

At parties, Adam was often asked 'What do you do?' and he answered 'I travel'. It was a truthful answer because for ten years, that is indeed what he had done, travelled. Between 2000-10, the young Englishman wandered the earth, on wild and adventurous journeys. Yet how does one become a perpetual wanderer, a professional traveller? What events lead a man to leave everything he owns and knows to roam the world for a decade? What brings him back? In order to answer these questions, let us go back to the beginning, the very beginning.

It was a time when Adam was choosing where to be born, a place where he may lead a nomad's life. There was only one stipulation, laid down by the great oneness, he must be born to a 'westernised' family, the implication of which was that it would be far harder to lead a nomadic lifestyle, harder that is, in a modern world - as opposed to remote parts of Africa, Asia or even Europe. Nevertheless, this was his lot, this was the way and the path Adam must walk.

Take my hand and rest a while and I will take you on a journey, into the world of a wanderer, but please hold on tightly, for we shall barely pause for breath.

The new spirit looked out over the universe, through the timelessness of his soul, the blue planet caught his eye again. Soon he would have to decide where he would be born, even now he was tempted to choose one of the other planets, perhaps one of the deep green ones again, far away in another space. He would not be human there or know the perils of having a body, yet there were different lessons for the spirit to learn. However, souls were queuing up to go to earth at this time, the beginning of the 1970s. It was a tough course to follow, but the rewards were high. He would have to choose within the next few thoughts, a gap was appearing for him. The fresh spirit had been waiting for the right parents, in order to play out the lessons he must learn on earth.

Gap, he thought.

He was thinking about the recent human habit of taking time out, a gap year and knew that in order to fulfil all his tasks on earth this time, he would have to engineer some sort of extension to the concept of gap years. Sometimes a gap year was just not enough, he would need many, a gap life perhaps. Consecutive gap years, in order to walk the difficult path he had chosen.

He watched the parents who would have this baby, it would be a second boy to follow the one who had already been born. He looked at the setting, a farm in the south of England. They were young strong parents, high spirited and adventurous. The free spirit emptied his mind, cleared any trace of intentions from his thoughts and glowed like a small star, like the millions of others waiting to be born, unseen by most humans. He could go anywhere that his imagination allowed him to - where the thought goes, the energy flows, but it was not a time to travel the many other parts of the Universe that he so enjoyed. His mind must be empty now, just a spark in the ether. He had two thoughts left to use.

Firstly. Shall I go to the green planet or the blue planet?
Secondly. This could be my last incarnation. Earth will not be a smooth path for me, yet it is where I will truly know the nature of the 'free spirit' and complete my lessons.

He was pulled to the blue and must trust the attraction that he felt. There was a moment's hesitation as his spirit prepared for the change, once he had made the move, the young human would not consciously remember anything about the time before he was born for another decade. He would feel a missing, yes, a longing feeling to be back somewhere, but the young one would not know what or where that place was. Now he must decide.

It must be earth, I must go there. ....***End of preview***

Also by A. Greenman:

The Practical Guide to Wwoofing:
World Wide Opportunities on Organic Farms

A Greenmans Short Stories

How to Take a Gap Life:
Sometimes a Gap Year is Just Not Enough!

The Wisdom of Travel
Words to Inspire

The Practical Guide to Wwoofing 2012

Volunteering with **WWOOF**

'World Wide Opportunities on Organic Farms'

"Accessibly and humanly written - it almost reads itself to you!"
Sue Coppard, W.w.o.o.f Founder

By A. Greenman

The Practical Guide to Wwoofing

Whist A. Greenman made his way around the world, between 2000-10, he often volunteered with the organisation - W.W.O.O.F (*World Wide Opportunities/ Willing Workers on Organic Farms*) who offer a chance to learn about working with the earth and nature, whilst helping out in any one or more of the venues situated in 100 countries around the world, in exchange for food and accommodation.

This is a simple *A-Z* type book about how to do it, filled with anecdotes from the veteran wwoofer. When released in 2009, the guide was praised by the founder of Wwoof, *Sue Coppard*, who said it was:

"A delightful and informative book, humanly and very accessibly written
- it almost reads itself to you!"

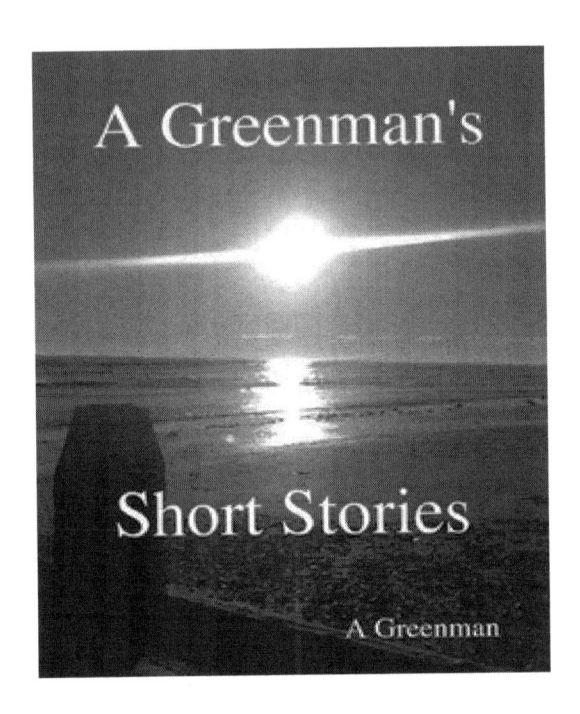

Can Blind Girls Travel?
Kate wants to see the world, only she cannot, for she is blind, and seeks to find a way how.

The Nature of London
Omar tires of his daily commute and longs for peace and quiet and to spend more time in his Victorian walled garden

The Spell of the Word Brand
Brand words come into our lives as softly as the morning dawn, but do we know what power they have on our lives?

Walking in the Clouds
A true story based on A.Greenman's own experience of a treacherous expedition to Snowdonia National Park, Wales.

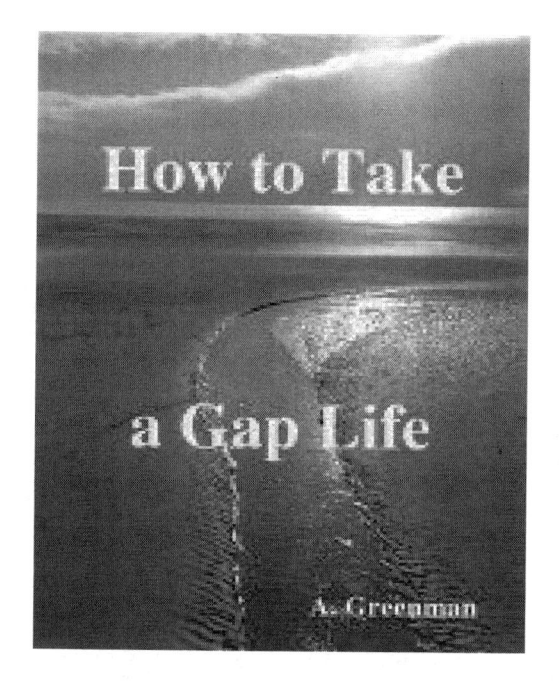

How to Take a Gap Life is a nomad's CV. Joseph took some time out, only sometimes a gap year is just not enough. 10 years later, he found he had actually taken a 'GAP LIFE'. He also finds that he is a perfectly qualified 'gapster' to fill a gap as a travel writer for a newspaper who is advertising. He is required to submit a CV about his extreme adventures around the globe and then further details about his wanderings in England, Wales, Scotland, France, Spain, Hungary, India, Brazil and New Zealand, amongst other places. A must read short story for all up and coming backpackers, nomads and gap year proposers.

The Wisdom of Travel

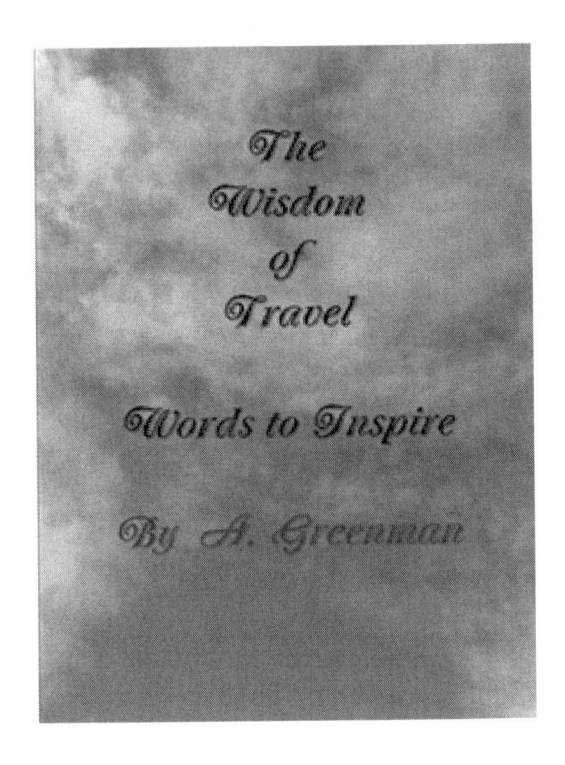

Words to Inspire

By A. Greenman

The verse of A. Greenman, taken from all of his work and put in one small booklet. With reflection on what may happen to us internally, as we embark on gap years, gap lives and serious time out from the daily grind, escaping the rat-race. Looking at the true nature of time and the nature of travel itself. A contemplative coffee break inspiration.

About the Author

A. Greenman was born in the south of England in 1971. He lives in Sussex, England, where he collects backpacks and future dreams.

For more information on the author; photos, public events, book signings, hardbacks, paperbacks and e-books, see:

www.greenmansbooks.com